SORRENTO AND THE AMALFI COAST

Published by KINA ITALIA

INTRODUCTION

Beautiful sea, lush vegetation, harsh, wild spurs of rock, steep cliffs dashed by waves that crash down into the crystal-clear water, a mild climate, a fascinating history and architectural monuments which still bear witness to it today, lively beaches and peaceful, unspoilt villages: all this and more is to be found on the Sorrento peninsula and the Amalfi coast.

It is no exaggeration to say that these are some of the loveliest and most interesting parts of Italy. A glimpse of the history of these areas is enough to see why, since time immemorial, they have exerted an unrivalled fascination on travellers and attracted an increasing number of visitors. The remains of magnificent Roman villas at Sorrento, Punta Campanella and Maiori bear witness to one of the earliest forms of tourism; patrician noblemen, delighted by the countless beauties of the peninsula, came to the area to put into practice the philosophical concept of otium (leisure) in these élite residences, built in some of the most enchanting, panoramic parts of the area. This irresistible attraction, which ebbed and flowed along with the area's tormented history, continued until the 17th century, when Sorrento, Amalfi and other major towns, like the archaeological sites of Herculaneum and Pompeii, became important destinations on the "Grand Tour" undertaken by aristocrats, writers and artists in general visiting the loveliest and most interesting sights in Italy. The 19th century saw a further increase in the numbers of travellers attracted by the charm of these lands; they left behind them magnificent villas, poetic sonnets, enthusiastic travel memoirs or paintings depicting the most picturesque spots, the brightest colours, the loveliest landscapes and the unique atmosphere of the peninsula, bearing witness to their love for these areas. Towards the end of the 19th century the tourists arriving here were still largely an élite, but with the development of hotels and the road network in the first half of this century, the Sorrento peninsula and the Amalfi coast finally became accessible to all.

As a result of the hard work and expertise of the local authorities and associations, the most important features of this area have been rediscovered (not that they had ever been forgotten!), especially in the last few decades. As well as the splendours of nature, these features include the history and tradition of the larger towns, with their glorious memories (like Amalfi, once a powerful maritime republic), and of the less well-known towns, whose history has been traced with patient research in order to give present-day visitors a detailed picture of these areas.

As a result, visits will no longer be restricted "merely" to the sea and the beaches, to walks through the picturesque lanes of fishing villages or terraces overflowing with citrus fruit groves and vineyards, or to an individual church or museum, but will become a sort of "full immersion", which combines various aspects (nature, history, architecture and folklore) without overlooking any of them, because it is only thus that the all-round character of the peninsula can be appreciated.

The sea represents the common denominator of the two sides of the peninsula (the Sorrento side and the Amalfi coast side), separated by the ridge formed by the Lattari mountains. Yet however beautiful and enchanting it may be, the sea alone cannot account for the true beauty of these areas, so different in appearance (flat and green on one side, harsh and impassable on the other because of the mountains sloping down to the water), and sometimes even in terms of architecture and history, yet imbued with the same undeniable charm.

Sorrento

Lying on a tufaceous terrace that slopes steeply down to the sea from a height of 50 metres, protected to the rear by the rocky spurs of the Lattari mountains, and immersed in the lush vegetation typical of the northern part of the Sorrento peninsula, Sorrento is one of the best-known and most popular resorts in Italy.

In the 18th century it was romantically dubbed "Sorrento the Kind", because of its mild climate and the unrivalled beauty of its site, but the essence of Sorrento is best expressed by its real name. The Latin Surrentum is associated with the myth of the sirens (inhabitants of these areas, according to legend), who sorely tempted even the valiant Ulysses with their sweet song. Like them, Sorrento, whose irresistible, multi-faceted beauty has cast its spell for centuries, still bewitches all who set eyes on it.

Its charm is unusual: it is a seaside town yet, because of its

1) Bathing beach and port
2) View
3) Typical Sorrento carriage

1) A characteristic lane
2) Limoncello liqueur shop
3) Inlay craftsman
4) The port
5) View and Punta Scutari
6) Marina Grande by night

raised position, it has no promenade; it maintains the picturesque character of the coastal towns, yet magnificent patrician villas are built there; it is bordered by crystal-clear waters and surrounded by enchanting gardens and citrus fruit groves, yet much of its beauty is to be found along the roads, stairways and passages cut into the rock which lead to the sea, in the houses with their typical local architecture, and in the monuments which testify to its long history.

The history of Sorrento is long indeed. Already inhabited in the Neolithic period, the town was probably built by the Teleboi, the ancient conquerors of Capri, and from that time on it became a desirable prey for all the populations who dominated the coastal areas at one time or another. Syracusans, Greeks and Samnites all played a part (for better or worse) in the town's history. Then came the Romans,

1) Church of S. Maria del Carmine
2-4) Inlay craftsmen
3) Fisherman
5) The port and bathing beach

who instituted a period of great prosperity, with systematic town planning, the building of the city walls and a construction boom, aided by an influx of patrician families from the capital who, especially in the Imperial age, spent their holidays in luxury homes built for them in Sorrento near the forum, the temples and public buildings.

An enchanting place, but also a strategic town because of its location, it subsequently met the fate of many other coastal towns, overrun successively by Goths, Byzantines, Lombards, Saracen pirates, Normans and so on, until the Bourbons and the "rediscovery" of Sorrento as an important destination on the 18th century gentleman's Grand Tour, followed by the upheavals of the 19th century which led to the Unification of Italy.

In the town centre, Piazza Torquato Tasso, dedicated to the great poet who was born in Sorrento in 1544, is the classic starting point for a visit to the town. As well as the monument to Tasso, the Piazza contains the statue of S. Antonino, the town's patron saint, and the attractive 18th century church of S. Maria del Carmine. The Cathedral, with the ruins of a Roman arch to its right, stands on the elegant, busy Corso Italia, the two branches of which separate here.

The Cathedral, which has ancient origins, was rebuilt in the 15th century and subsequently altered on many occasions (for example, the façade dates from 1924). The

1-2) View
3) Marina Grande

1) Bathing beach and port
2) View
3) Piazza Tasso

15

pronaos, with two ancient columns, and the lovely marble side door decorated with the Aragon coat of arms, date back to the 15th century alterations. The interior, divided into a nave and two aisles, contains some valuable 16th/17th century canvases and splendid 14th/15th century marble bas-reliefs, together with the archbishop's throne, which dates from 1573. The campanile preceding the cathedral, which rests on two

1) Monument to Torquato Tasso
2) Sedil Dominova
3) Sedil Dominova (16th c.)
4) Aerial view of Marina Grande

Romanesque arches supported by four ancient columns, is also interesting. Nearby, still on Corso Italia, stands the 13th century Palazzo Veniero, its magnificent façade decorated by arched openings and friezes in yellow and grey tufo. Continuing towards the sea from the Cathedral, we come to the Sedile Dominova, the monument which symbolises Sorrento. The elegant

1-2-3) Details of Marina
4) The port

18

1) **Typical outdoor café**
2) **Monument to S. Anthony Abate**
3) **Characteristic view**
4) **View**

square arched loggia was built in the 15th century as a nobleman's seat, and was crowned with a spectacular majolica-covered dome in the 17th century. Nearby is the Church of S. Francis of Assisi, whose small cloister is a jewel of late 14th century architecture. Two sides of the portico surrounding it have round arches resting on octagonal pillars, while the other two feature entwining arches of Arab style, supported by slender

columns with capitals of different orders.

On leaving the cloister, cross Piazza della Vittoria, where a few remains of an ancient Temple of Venus still stand, to the Villa Comunale, surrounded by a delightful public park and ornamented by a terrace overlooking the sea which offers a spectacular view of the gulf of Naples. From here, the visitor can follow the picturesque stairways down to the Marina Piccola port area or the Marina Grande beach, where the main bathing establishments are situated. The nearby Basilica of S. Antonino was probably built in the 11th century as an extension to an existing 9th century oratory dedicated to the patron saint, and then radically transformed in the early 17th century. It is ornamented by a magnificent 11th century portal with Corinthian capitals and fragments from an older post-and-lintel construction, and contains some outstanding 17th/18th century paintings and an interesting 18th

1) Villa Pompeiana: portico
2) Villa Pompeiana: interior
3) Villa Pompeiana: garden
4) Cloister of S. Francis' Monastery

century crib. From the church, Via Correale leads to the 18th century villa of the same name, an outstanding example of Neapolitan baroque, whose luxurious rooms contain the Museo Correale di Terranova. The museum houses an interesting collection of Greek, Roman and mediaeval marbles, mostly from the city's buildings, majolica and porcelain from the main European manufacturers, precious carved and inlaid Neapolitan furniture, major paintings by 17th and 18th century Italian and foreign artists (Luca Giordano, Sebastiano Conca, Jan Brueghel and Rubens) and 19th century landscapes. The works by leading representatives of the Posillipo school (Teodoro Duclère and Giacinto Gigante) are particularly outstanding.

1) S. Francis' Monastery
2) S. Francis Monastery: detail
3) View from Villa Pompeiana
4) View

) Marina Grande

2) Fishermen's boats at Marina Grande

1) The sea at Sorrento
2) Vesuvius seen
   from Sorrento
3) Hydroplane to Capri

1

2

3

31

1-2) Puolo Marina
3) Regina Giovanna baths
4) Ruins of the Roman villa
   of Pollius Felix

4

THE MUSEUM CORREALE

The museum was set up from a private foundation by the Correale brothers Alfredo and Pompeo, the Counts of Terranova. They were the last descendants of an old Sorrentine family and in their wills they made provision for Villa Correale and the art collections housed

1) Main façade of Museo Correale di Terranova
2) Entrance hall of Palazzo and garden
3) Francesco de Mura, Madonna and Child: oil on copper
4) Capodimonte porcelain group (18th c.)

there to be turned into a museum bearing their name. In addition to the art treasures and the building in which they are housed, this bequest also included the garden and a large area of farm land the produce of which is sold to contribute to the upkeep of the museum. Set up as an institution with the royal decree of February 18, 1904, the museum was opened to the public on May 10, 1942. The collections are laid out on three floors in 24 rooms plus the attic, which has recently been renovated for use as an exhibiting area.

1) Showcase in room 9 with collection of oriental porcelain
2) Pair of centre tables with tortoiseshell tops (18th c.)

Photographs supplied by SORRENTO CINEFOTO CLUB

1) Giacinto Gigante room

2) Archaeological Section and "Augustus' Base"

**1) "Mirror room": Neapolitan furnishings
dating from second half of 17th c.**

**2) Francesco Celebrano (Naples 1724-1812):
The Game "Odds and Evens"**

MARQUETRY

Sorrento, home of Tasso, known as the land of the Sirens because of its rich orange and lemon-tree orchards, is also a city of art. It was made thus by the Artisans whose patient and often obscure daily toil has, since the nineteenth century, given rise to Sorrentine marquetry-work, with furniture which has crossed the borders of the peninsula to make the name of Sorrento known even in the most distant places. The architect Alessandro Fiorentino has documented this long tradition, in an attempt to spread ever further knowledge about yew-wood marquetry. In the eighties, in addition to a publication, he also presented a travelling exhibition which brought to Paris, Cologne, Lilles, Nantes and New York a wealth of information about Sorrentine marquetry of the nineteenth century as well as the architect's own modern designs. The tables of Luigi Gargiulo, also presented in the Palazzo Reale of Naples and Caserta, the shelves of Grandville and Giuseppe Gargiulo, the inlaid furniture in ebony and ivory of Francesco Grandi and the inlaid frames of Almerico Gargiulo are among the most important documents of nineteenth century work. The period marked the apex of Sorrentine artistic production. To this tradition is linked the inlaid furniture of Alessandro Fiorentino, whose work mirrors the artistry and technical expertise of the

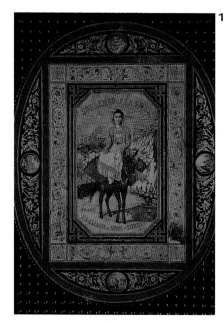

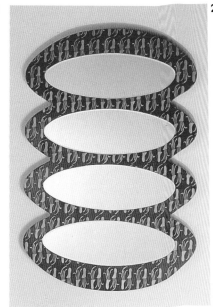

1) Inlaid table top with figure of woman in Sorrento costume
2) The first mirror, mirror on the wall. Designer: Luigi Fiorentino
3) Positano chair. Designer: Alessandro Fiorentino

4 Sorrento artisans as a constant, supporting the object in its modern design.

Organisation of inlay-work has remained unchanged by time and is carried out by a number of different specialists. The designers supply the design which then goes to the inlayer who is responsible for the fretwork. The latter, the key element in the entire production cycle, is seated behind the fretting machine and a rigid horizontal piane on which he guides the veneer block, with the design to be inlaid, around a small vertical saw; moving his hands in steady rhythmical movements. The woods most often used for veneer, in thicknesses of tenths of a millimetre, are ebonised pearmaple, orange wood and a whole series of coloured woods. All the inlaid pieces are then fixed with glue by the assembler onto a cardboard support, so that all the decoration can be transferred by the inlayer as a covering for the object that the carpenter has built. Then begins the final stage of decoration, carried out by the "finisher", who completes and touches up the details, making precise and very fine Indian inktraces along the various inlaid moulds. The work is finished after the hinges, locks and upholstery have been applied, with the varnishing of the objects, which used to be done using buffers and rubber spray.

5

4) Cigar box
5) Inlaid table: Il Mellonaro

Photographs supplied by (1-4):
architect ALESSANDRO FIORENTINO

Massa lubrense

A seaside resort at the tip of the Sorrento peninsula, Massalubrense is also an important agricultural centre, especially for olives and oranges, because the gently sloping land on which it is built is particularly fertile. The splendour of the surrounding countryside and the spectacular view of the Isle of Capri, which lies right opposite in the crystal-clear waters of the sea, would alone make it worth a visit. However, Massalubrense also holds other beauties in store, associated with its historical and artistic treasures. The most outstanding is the Church of S. Maria delle Grazie, once a cathedral, built in the early 16th century in one of the most panoramic spots of the town. The lovely painting with the effigy of the Virgin Mary, housed in the apse, dates back to the time of its construction, while the exquisite majolica floor of the transept and presbytery was laid during reconstruction work in the 18th century. The sanctuary of S. Maria della Lobra at Marina della Lobra, the pretty lower part of the town, containing its small port, also dates from the 16th century.

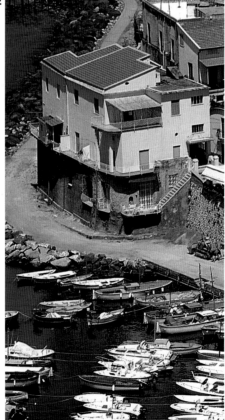

1) The port
2-3-4) The Marina

Positano

The ancient seaside town lies on the southern side of the Lattari Mountains, sloping down gently towards the sea on terraces constructed along the rock spurs of M. Comune and M. Sant'Angelo a Tre Pizzi, right in the middle of the gulf between Punta Germano to the west and Capo Sottile to the east. Probably founded by a group of inhabitants of Paestum, who survived the destruction of their city by the Saracens around the 10th century, the town was built around the ancient Benedictine Abbey of S. Vito. It soon became a major maritime power, representing serious cause for concern even to the powerful Republic of Amalfi.
Because of its outstanding panoramic position and mild climate, together with its

1) **Characteristic spot**
2) **Typical architecture**
3) **Corner of Positano**

picturesque architecture and the lush surrounding countryside, Positano has become one of the most popular resorts on the Amalfi coast. Its simple white houses with their characteristic vaulted roofs, standing out amid the myriad colours of splendid gardens or shaded by exotic palm trees, its historical beauties and the spectacular blue sea have constituted an irresistible attraction since the turn of the century, when tourism began to develop in the area.

The winding Via Pasitea, the main road which leads towards Piazza Flavio Gioia with its exceptional view, runs right across the town, also crossed by picturesque

1-2) The Marina
3) View

44

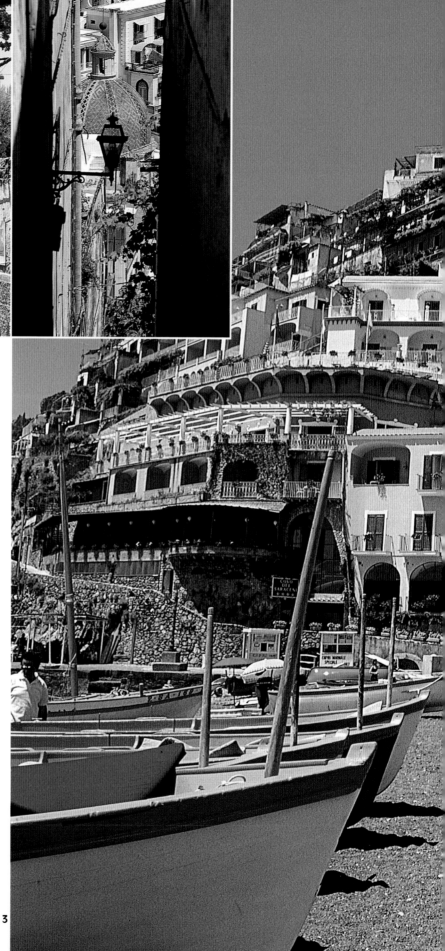

stepped lanes. The beauty of this area was recognised as early as Roman times, when a magnificent villa was built, of which interesting remains still survive. In the piazza stands the Parish Church of S. Maria Assunta, easily identifiable by its majestic majolica-covered dome and the separate campanile, which features an outstanding medieval bas-relief portraying sea creatures and a fox. The Parish Church is built on the remains of an older church; significant fragments of the mosaic decorations of the original building are still visible in the interior, which is divided into a nave and two aisles by sturdy pillars.

In addition to the paintings, mostly dating from the 18th century, which decorate the

1-2-3) Characteristic views

1-2-3-4) Around Positano
5) Panoramic view of beach

various altars with their coloured marble facing, the 13th century panel in the Byzantine manner on the high altar, depicting the Virgin and Child, is noteworthy. The vestry contains the precious Reliquary of S. Vitus, which dates back to the early 16th century. On leaving the church, the visitor can follow the seaward direction down to Marina Grande, the large beach ringed by cliffs from which the Capri ferry departs. There is an unrivalled view from here, across the entire gulf as far as the two furthermost headlands. There are other lovely beaches to the west of the town (Fornillo) and to the east (La Porta,

1-2) The Marina
3) View
4) The beach

Ciumicello and Arienzo).
Fascinating relics of local community life in the Palaeolithic and Mesolithic eras (various household objects and weapons) have been found in a cave near one of these beaches (La Porta). In addition to the attractions offered by the town of Positano, some pleasant excursions can be made in its immediate neighbourhood; for example, in the direction of Montepertuso and Nocella, two small towns that can also be reached on foot, in which the characteristic atmosphere of the picturesque inland towns remains almost intact, or the longer and more difficult trips to M. Sant'Angelo a Tre Pizzi and M. Comune. The first of these mountains offers the fascinating sight of a natural arch hollowed out in a spike of rock.

1-3) Panoramic views
2) Night scene
4) View and beach

Nearby, the small church of S. Pietro on the headland of the same name is worth a visit, especially for the splendid view it offers. Starting from the Positano observation point behind Fornillo beach, visitors can follow the road that leads along a section of the coast intersected by spectacular cliffs, rising sheer out of the sea, to the picturesque Ponte dei Libri (Book Bridge), so called because the rock walls present incredibly regular stratification, reminiscent of the pages of giant books.

1) **Night scene**
2-3) **Panoramic views**

1

1-2-3) Details
4) The beach

1-2-3) Sections of the Amalfi coast
4) Sunset seen from the coast, with
Capri and the Faraglioni rocks
in the background

60

4

Praiano

Behind Capo Sottile, on the far slopes of Mount Tre Cavalli, and looking eastwards, there is the little town of Praiano. Once an old fishing village it is now a popular seaside resort with hotels and camping facilities that can accomodate large numbers of tourists. The parish church, dedicated to Saint Luke, is found in the upper part of the town, in a spot with a lovely view; the church houses a precious silver figure of Saint Luke. Praiano's beach is the small, enchanting Marina di Praia, which is found at the end of the wild Praia valley. The surrounding cliffs have been deeply marked by erosion. On a rocky promonotory stands the cylindrical mass of the Torre a Mare, a medieval structure which recalls the centuries-old struggle of the area's inhabitants against the attacks of pirates.

1-2) Enchanting views

1) Church of S. Gennaro at Vettica
   Maggiore
2) Typical ceramic dome
3) Section of coast near Praiano

Furore

This small town, between Praiano and Conca dei Marini, mainly owes its fame to the deep gorge from which it takes its name, one of the cracks which occasionally slice inland through the continuous line of rock spurs running along the entire Amalfi coast. The few houses in Furore, often isolated, are scattered over the sloping land on which the local crops, olives and grapes, are grown. Beyond the gorge, a road offering spectacular views over the coast and the sea leads inland to the Agerola plateau. Situated 650 metres above sea level, this lovely countryside, in which extensive fields alternate with thick woods ornamented by streams and orchards, is the ideal place for those who enjoy quiet, relaxing walks. Beyond the town of Agerola are the nearby resorts of Bomerano, with its interesting little church, and San Lazzaro, with an observation point which offers an outstanding view of the Amalfi coast.

1) Sunset
2) The "Madonnina" on the Positano-Amalfi road
3) The Furore fjord
4) Furore beach

Conca dei Marini

This is a little town of ancient origins composed of a compact nucleus of houses, nestling on the slope which forms the spur of Capo Conca. Probably founded in the early centuries of the Christian era, Conca dei Marini underwent considerable development in the Middle Ages, when its merchant fleet enjoyed commercial relations with the major ports on the Mediterranean.

Capo di Conca extends out to the open sea with a hook-shaped spur, on which stands the Conca Tower, built in '500 as a lookout post and first line of defence against the frequent attacks of pirates. Until recently, the Tower also served as a cemetry for the inhabitants of Conca dei Marini. From the Tower one can see a beautiful, wide panorama; looking east to Capo d'Orso, west to Capo Sottile, beyond which the "Li Gialli" crags rise up from the sea and, further on Punta Campanella and the unmistakable outline of Capri.

The western side of the little peninsula which forms Capo di Conca encloses a charming bay where the deep limpid sea has a particularly attractive crystalline colour, an ideal destination for a boat trip.

1) Conca headland and bay
2) Sunset
3) The Emerald Grotto
4) The town

68

Amalfi

Amalfi, Italy's oldest maritime republic, is set on the coast where the Valle dei Mulini descends to the sea. The first impression of the city, arriving by land or sea, is that of a quiet seaside resort, with its quaint white houses scattered about the narrow alluvial plain and the surrounding hillsides, periodically taken over by crowds of tourists. An ancient legend tells how in the 4th century A.D., the Romans, on their way to Constantinople - which had just become the capital of the empire - were shipwrecked int he Adriatic near what was then Epidaurus- and is now Cavtat

1) **Night scene**
2) **Partial view of town seen from port**
3) **The port**
4) **Typical Moorish architecture**

3

(from Civitas) - in Dalmatia. When the survivors put to sea they changed course and settled permanently near Palinuro. Here they founded the city of MELPHE, and came to be known as the MELPHITANI. Later, when they had colonized the area which is now Eboli, they built a new city on the coast further north, and this was named"A-Melphitani" or "city of those who came from Melphe" A-MELPHE. However, historical data indicate that this area was inhabited even during the Roman empire, and proof of this can be found in several marble fragments and remains of buildings dating back to that period.

Amalfi is mentioned in official documents from the 8th century onwards.

It almost certainly underwent a period of Byzantine rule after Narsete's victory over the Ostrogoths in 573; there are also good grounds for believing that the conflicts during that period have rise to Amalfi's maritime activities, if only in terms of supplies, though it is difficult to say to what extent.

The city did, however (with the aid of Byzantine Naples) succeed in holding back and in finally defeating the siege between 785 and 788, by Arechi, prince of Benevento and a powerful Longobard duke.

Because of the distance, economic problems and political conflicts which separated Constantinople from Amalfi, the latter which was growing increasingly richer and more powerful, was soon able to govern its affairs almost autonomously, and even succeeded in routing Arab contingents during an expedition sent out in 812 by the Imperial patricians of Sicily.

This new-found wealth and substantial political autonomy sparked off internal struggles and Sicardo, the ambitious Longobard duke of Benevento, treacherously occupied and sacked the city (in 838 or 837), deporting many of its inhabitants to Longobard Salerno.

Fortunately, these dark days soon came to an end. Sicardo was murdered by conspirators and the citizens of Amalfi returned to their city after a year's deportation, thanks to a daring attack which led to the conquest and sack of Salerno (in 839 or 840). This experience led the citizens to elect a ruler, bestowing on him the title of count. This marked the beginning of the second golden period in the history of Amalfi, which was by now a free and powerful Republic. After the period of the counts, the city was governed by two Rectors, and then by two Prefects (which were probably both names for the same office), who were reelected annually, and subsequently ruled for longer periods.

The institutions then created the figure of the Judges, whom the Eastern emperor named Imperial Patricians.

This led in 897 to the proclamation of a DOGE or dukeas supreme magistrate - and that is why Amalfi came to be known as a duchy, at least until the end of the 16th century. Constantinople's approval of the doge elected by the people was little more than a formality as Amalfi had, by that time, its own laws magistrates and currency. The Republic stretched along the northern coast of the gulf of Salerno as far as the crest of the Lattarian Mountains, the territory of Sorrento in the west and Salerno in the east. To the north beyond the mountainous ridge, the Republic ruled over Lettere and Gragnano as far as the borders of the duchy of Naples. Thus, from the 9th century onwards, Amalfi's fleet had a

1) **View and cathedral**
2) **Partial view**

strong influence over the political developments in Southern Italy, intervening in local disputes and defeating - together with the fleets from Naples and Gaeta - the Arab forces at Ostia in 849, as they were about to set off to conquer Rome.

After the battle, the Arab fleet was overcome and scattered by a violent storm. Under the protection of the Carolingian emperor, Ludovic II, who was recognized as its sovereign ruler, Amalfi sent its fleet to the island of San Salvatore (now Castel dell'Ovo) to free Anastasio, bishop of Naples, who had been imprisoned there by Duke Sergio. As a reward for its decisive intervention, the city obtained, in the same year (872), sovereignty over Capri.

The Republic's foreign policy, which reflected a desire to protect the commercial and maritime interests of its citizens preserved the city's neutrality for long periods during the conflicts between the various Christian powers, and during their more or less united attempts to overthrow the Islamic powers. In 1920, however, Amalfi fought in Calabria alongside the Longobards to free Reggio from the Arabs.

Amalfi reached the height of its wealth and power in that fatal year, 1000 by which time it had warehouses in Con-stantinople, Alexandria, Cyprus, Beirut, Jaffa, Laodicea, Tripoli in Syria and in many other ports. The goods imported from the East included perfumes, textiles and precious fabrics, carpets and spices. Collection and trading centres for these products were dotted around southern Italy and particularly in Naples, Salerno, Taranto, Barletta, Catania, Syracusa and Mazara whilst on the mainland, there were centres in Benevento, Capua, Francavilla and Cosenza. Churches were built

overseas, just as in the Holy Land, and alms-houses and hospitals were set up for the pilgrims, with efficient health services and medical structures which were way ahead of their times. Neither should it be forgotten that the celebrated Order of the Knights of Malta was founded by one of the Amalfi's citizens. It was Fra' Gerardo Sasso of Scala who in 1020 founded the Order of the Knights Hospitallers or Knights of St. John of Jerusalem.

The Knights Hospitallers ran the hospital and church of St.John of Jerusalem and as the work of the hospital was extended to other countries, they became known as the Knights of Rhodes, and finally as the Knights of Malta.

Even today the Maltese coat-of-arms bears the characteristic "swallow-tail" cross of Amalfi, which is also the official badge of the sovereign Military Order of Malta in Rome.

In the Municipio in Amalfi, there are still the"Amalfi Tables" and although these do not appear in the original edition, they nevertheless constitute an extremely important juridical document, as they represented maritime law in the Mediterranean area for many centuries.

Renewed internal conflicts led to the fall of the republic and to the gradual decline of its wealth and commercial activities.

History began to repeat itself and in 1039 Guaimario IV, prince of Salerno, conquered the duchies of Amalfi and Sorrento. But this time it was the Normans who took over the city in 1073, led by Robert Guiscard.

During Norman rule in the south, Amalfi was guaranteed a certain amount of autonomy.

There were still occasional out-breaks of ancient pride and displays of its former power in 1087, for example, Pantaleone di Mauro, a nobleman from Amalfi,

led a combined naval expedition of ships from the fleets of Pisa, Genoa and Amalfi, against Tunis, which was ruled by Bey Timin. Our gallant commander also received honours for his good works in both public and religious spheres. It was he who commissioned the decorated bronze doors from Constantinople for the two mother-churches in Atrani and Amalfi.

For a short period the Republic even succeeded in winning back its former independence, but it had by then reached the end of its glorious history.

In 1096, during the first crusade of the Holy Sepulchre, Amalfi once more became independent, only to be conquered by Roger I in 1101, although it succeeded in preserving a certain amount of administrative autonomy.

The Normans returned to the attack once they had consolidated their power after Amalfi's refusal to surrender its fortresses: Roger I laid siege to the city and captured it on February 17, 1131.

Pisa also took advantage of these favourable circumstances to attack Amalfi by sea in 1135, and again in 1137, sacking and laying waste the whole area: Atrani was almost completely destroyed, while Ravello, Scala, Minori, Maiori and Amalfi were seriously damaged.

In addition to valuable furnishings, art and culture were also part of the booty - including Justinian's laws or "Pandects" - which are now kept in the Biblioteca Laurenziana in Florence.

1) **View and port**
2) **The beach**

1) View
2-3-4) Typical architecture

Having irretrievably lost its independence and political importance in international affairs, the city began to increase its trade and maritime activities, winning back some of its former prestige in the commercial field. And this, of course, was looked upon very favourably by the ruling dynasties in Naples, who were represented in Amalfi by a Strategist or Stratigoth, as in Salerno and Messina.

The sea, which was the fount of life and prosperity in Amalfi, was also responsible for some of the worst disasters that ever hit the city - especially those in 1013 and 1270.

On November 24, 1343 a seaquake submerged and wiped out a third of the city: the whole of the port was destroyed together with the arsenals and ships, and the city walls and buildings along the coast were all washed away. Petrarch, who was in Naples during that period, recorded the event in one of his "Epistles".

The city never recovered and fell into decline.

At the end of the 14th century, it was subjected by a San Severino (Venceslao) and later became the fief of Giordano Colonna in 1405 and of Raimondo del Balzo Orsini in 1438.

The frequent change in feudal lords seemed to be an indication of the city's continuing importance, bestowing upon it a kind of posthumous stamp of nobility.

In 1461, Ferdinand I, King of Naples, gave the city as a dowry to his natural daughter Maria, when she married Ferdinando Piccolomini, and Amalfi was ruled by the family for over a century until 1582. Amalfi's history after that date is reduced to the everyday events of a small fishing and agricultural centre, which carried on its ancient crafts and industrial activities (production of

1) View of port
2) Ceramic portraying a chart of the East Mediterranean
3) Statue of Flavio Gioia
4) The beach
5) View and cathedral

5 paper, rigging and fishing nets) until it was swept by the wave of tourism.

1

2

3

THE DUOMO

The monumental Duomo or cathedral towers over a steep flight of steps, and is dedicated to Sant'Andrea. It was founded in the 9th century, extended in 987 and later in 1203, rebuilt in the Arab-Norman style which is typical of Sicilian architecture. It underwent alterations in 1526, 1566 and 1691 and was completely rebuilt in 1701 to 1731, this time in baroque style. The animated extremely scenographic façade was a later addition and was rebuilt between 1875 and 1894, after the previous façade collapsed in 1861. It was the work of Enrico Alvino (Milan, 1809-72) and, after his death, of the Neapolitan architects, Luigi della Corte and Guglielmo Raimondi, who drew their inspiration from primitive 13th century designs, rare ancient fragments and written memoirs. The façade is crowned by a high gable with a mosaic decoration showing Christ on the throne

1) S. Andrew's fountain
2) Piazza Duomo (Cathedral square)
3) Night scene
4) Partial view of Borgo Marinaro
5) Detail of cathedral façade
6) Typical carriage, and ceramic by Diodoro Cossa portraying the history of Amalfi

between the symbols of the Evangelists and earthly powers, based on a drawing the well-known Neapolitan painter, Domenico Morelli (1826-1901). To the left of the façade is the beautiful, tall bell-tower dating back to 1180, but in fact completed a century later, in 1276. It has cylindrical corner turrets linked to one another and to the cylindrical spire by Arabian-style arches, and is surmounted by a small lantern and covered in bright yellow and green majolica tiles. Unlike the turrets, the base and body of the tower are parallelepipedal; the four sides are divided by level-marking cornices and decorated with mullioned windows with two lights on the bottom floor, and three lights on the upper floor. The steps in front of the Duomo lead into the atrium, decorated with bands of black and white marble, and supported by columns. The lunette over the main entrance has a fresco of our Lady of the Assumption by Paolo Vetri (Enna, 1855-1937) painted after a design by Morelli. The frescoes on each side of the atrium have the following themes on the left, Jesus sleeping in the boat on the lake during the storm and Jesus talking to the crowd from the boat; and on the right, the calling of Peter and Andrew and the miraculous haul of fishes. These frescoes from 1929 were also the work of Vetri after sketches by Morelli.The wonderful bronze door of the main entrance is very old, extremely well preserved and a true masterpiece of art and skilfull craftsmanship. It dates back to before 1066 and,

according to the inscription, was cast in Constantinople under the supervision of Simon of Syria, and donated to the Duomo by Pantaleone di Mauro, head of the Amalfian colony in the capital of the Byzantine empire. Each door is divided into 24 panels.The four centre panels, showing Christ, the Virgin Mary (with initials in Greek letters) St. Peter and St. Andrew, were made using a mixed technique, in which enamel and niello were blended with paint.The fifth series of panels (from the top) is composed of six lion's head plates. The lions have bronze rings in their jaws like doors, whilst the remaining metal plates in the panel have relief decorations of crosses and grapevines and are secured to the doors with bronze nails.The

marble door-jambs are also richly decorated with foliage, lions, birds and spiral motifs, and the lintel, decorated with acanthus leaves, is a very old, valuable fragment taken from an older building.The cathedral interior was basically rebuilt in the 18th century even though the marble which covers the ancient columns (the seventh on the left and right) was completed in 1827 by the Neapolitan marble-workers Giuseppe and Tommaso Borelli. The interior now appears in its baroque "edition"with a double row of ten columns dividing the three naves of the ancient church built in the shape of the Latin cross. The transept and central nave have a fine caisson ceiling made in 1702 by the carvers Francesco Gori, Santolo and Ludovico d'Angelo

1) **Detail of cathedral portico**
2) **The cathedral**

on a design by Michelangelo Guglielmelli. The painted sections were the work of Andrea dell'Asta. The major works of art, starting from the right, include:
- in the first chapel, a valuable early 16th century marble altar piece with three Saints;
- at the far end of the nave, where it meets the transept, the tomb of Bishop Andrea d'Acunto, who died in 1503 and who was honoured with the name "Pater Patrie" for his good works;
- at the far end of the transept, the "Choir" chapel, which contains various reliquaries and busts of saints.
At the entrance to the presbytery, we can admire two ancient monolithic columns with capitals similar to those of the

1) Cathedral crypt: S. Andrew's skull
2) Cathedral interior: detail of nave
3) Altar with statues by Pietro Bernini
4) Various fragments from Roman and Medieval periods housed in the Paradise Cloister

ambo in Salerno, and two candelabra with mosaic decorations. Two lavish mosaic 12 to 13th century pulpits stand on each side of the high altar. These are two of the few surviving masterpieces from the medieval cathedral like the baptismal font in red Egyptian porphyry which is kept in the first chapel on the left. A flight of steps between the fourth and fifth chapels on the right leads down to the fascinating Crypt. This dates back to the 13th century, and was built to house the relics of Sant'Andrea Apostolo, protector of the Republic, which were brought to Amalfi in 1206 from Constantinople, following events linked to the unfortunate 4th crusade. The crypt has two naves with pointed cross vaults resting on four columns, which were later turned into pillars and covered in marble. It was restored by the good offices of the king of Spain, Philip III in 1600-1612; the marble statues of San Stefano and San Lorenzo are by Pietro Bernini (Sesto Fiorentino, 1562-1629), father and teacher of the more famous Gian Lorenzo Bernini.

Almost a century later the translation of St. Andrew's body from Constantinople (or, as some scholars would have it, from Patras) a peculiar oily substance was seen to exude from the bones of the saint. Known as "St. Andrew's manna", it was said to have miraculous properties. The Cappella del Crocefisso can be reached through a door between the 1st and 2nd chapels in the left nave, or directly from the atrium at the front of the duomo, through a carved doorway in the bottom left hand corner. The "Chapel of the Crucifix" was the original name of the Duomo, and this chapel has also preserved the original architectonic structure of the ancient cathedral. It was restored in 1938 to eliminate the baroque additions, and to uncover two of the three original naves, the mullioned windows with two and three lights, and the few surviving traces of frescoes. The richly decorated capitals of the columns support raised ogival arches which are developed into a gallery with double mullioned windows resting on smaller pairs of columns.

CLOISTERS

The atrium in the Duomo also leads to the lovely Chiostro del Paradiso (Paradise Cloister) an elegant Arabian-style structure built in 1266- 68 as a cemetery for Amalfi's most important citizens. It was abandoned in the early 17th century and restored in 1908 along with various relics from Roman and medieval times. It is composed of pairs of small columns supporting pointed interwoven arches. The distinctly oriental flavour is emphasised by the palm trees in the shady garden in the middle. Leaving the duomo in the direction of Via Genova and Via Capuano, leading

1-2) Paradise Cloister
   and cathedral campanile
3) Paradise Cloister
4) Paradise Cloister: Christ giving His
   blessing (13th century)
5) Cloister of Franciscan Monastery
   (13th c.), now Hotel Luna

inland, we follow the Torrente Chiairito (or Canneto on the left, which has cut deep into the mountain side, flowing through citrus-groves and creating bubbling waterfalls and rapids. The most picturesque spot is at the Mulino Rovinato (ruined Mill). Once the mills were an important feature of industrial activity, one of the oldest industries in Europe; paper making began in the Valle dei Mulini, following contacts between the inhabitants of Amalfi and the Arab peoples.This kind of industry required a large amount of water both for soaking raw materials and for processing, and in addition, provided an abundant supply of energy. Returning towards the coast down Corso Roma and Via Amendola, we reach the Tower of Amalfi, which stands on a promontory and was one of the numerous ancient look-out points in the city. A visit to the hotel allows us to enjoy yet another characteristic panorama. The Luna hotel was once, in fact, the site of an ancient Franciscan monastery, and we can still see the old 13th century cloister with its tall, pointed arches supported by alternating double and single columns, and the well in the centre of the courtyard. It was here, in 1879, that the famous Norwegian Playwright, Henrik Ibsen, wrote his masterpiece, "A Doll's House".

5

REGATTA OF THE ANCIENT MARITIME REPUBLICS

This is one of the most spectacular events held in Amalfi, combining folklore and festival with the history and splendours of the powerful maritime republics of the past: Amalfi, Genoa, Pisa and Venice. Although the idea was originally conceived in the Forties, the boat race was first held in Pisa in 1956, and since then has been hosted in turn by one of the four competing cities every year. The boats, built in Venice by the Gondoliers' Cooperative, have eight oarsmen and a cox, and are decorated by splendid wooden figureheads, each with the symbol of the Republic to which the boat belongs: a winged horse

1-2) Pageant

for Amalfi, a winged dragon for Genoa, an eagle for Pisa and a lion for Venice. A particularly interesting event is the pageant, in which each city portrays an important episode of its history. Amalfi stages the marriage of Duke Giovanni II to Duchess Maria, accompanied by judges, ambassadors and knights of Malta, and a host of pages, bridesmaids and buglers. All the participants wear magnificent costumes, identical to the originals right down to the smallest detail.

1) Regatta of the Maritime Republics
2-3) Characters in pageant

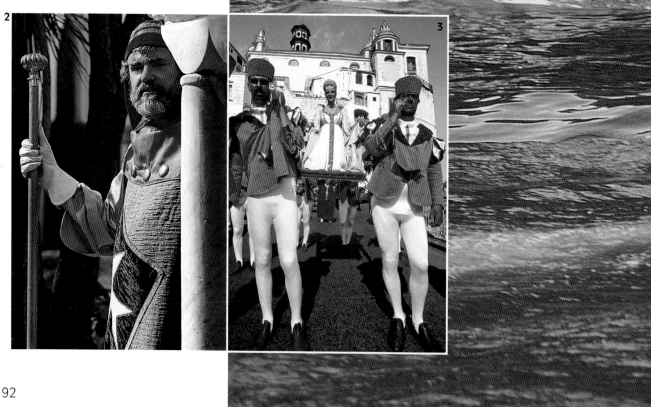

VALLE DEI MULINI, AMALFI

Valle dei Mulini (Water-Mill Valley), situated just inland of the town, is one of the most interesting and enjoyable resorts in the Amalfi district. From the cathedral square, follow Via Genova, then continue inland along Via Capuano. After crossing modern districts and leaving the town, continue along the left bank of the Chiarito River to Valle dei Mulini. The rather harsh landscape is softened by numerous vineyards and citrus fruit groves, and the valley, with its myriad of streams, is teeming with little waterfalls. Because of the practically unlimited water supply, numerous paper mills, among the oldest in Europe, were built in the area in the past; some were actually founded in the Middle Ages. Ranging in size from cottage industries to large industrial complexes, they exploited the area's water for various production processes (especially pulping wood), often using the water-mills after which the valley is named. The prettiest of these mills is the Mulino Rovinato (Ruined Mill). The paper manufacturing tradition became widespread in the Amalfi area because of the Republic's trade with the Arabs, skilled practitioners of this art since ancient times. It remained firmly established in Valle dei Mulini throughout the 19th century, and in some cases continued into the 20th, as demonstrated by the industrial structures still existing.

1) Winged horse
2) Paper Museum: press

2 The Paper Museum (Museo della Carta), housed in an old paper mill, is a particularly interesting source of information about this local tradition and the various manufacturing techniques used over the centuries. In addition to engravings and prints, paper manufacturing machines from different periods are on display at the museum.

3 AGRICULTURAL HISTORY MUSEUM

Inaugurated in 1989 at Valle dei Mulini on the occasion of the 38th Regatta of the Ancient Maritime Republics, the Agricultural History Museum (Museo della Civiltà Contadina) offers an interesting insight into Amalfi's agriculture over the past four centuries. Among the most interesting exhibits are a 17th century screw press, wine casks, various cereal grinding mills, a 19th century walnut spinning-wheel, still in working order, and the characteristic chestnut wood baskets still used for the grape harvest.

1) Paper Mill Valley
2) Paper Museum: pulping equipment
3) Agricultural History Museum:
    sundry tools

1

THE AMALFI CIVIC MUSEUM

Housed in the Town Hall building, the Civic Museum (Museo Civico) contains numerous relics of Amalfi's history, including paintings (such as some very interesting sketches by Domenico Morelli for the great mosaic in the cathedral, which portrays Christ enthroned among the symbols of the evangelists and the earthly powers), city banners, historical costumes for the regatta pageants, religious vestments and various treasures. The museum's pride and joy is the famous Tabula Amalphitana, the code containing the maritime trade laws of the Amalfi Republic, first drawn up in the 11th-12th century.

2

1) View of Morelli room
2) The Tabula Amalphitana
3-4-5) Panoramic views

Ravello

The town, where the natural beauty and the splendid landscape combine with the peace and enchantment of the precious architectural monuments, the villas and gardens, is one of the most famous and popular locations on the Amalfi coast.

The most ancient documentation on Ravello dates back to the ninth century, when the town came under Amalfi. Taken over by Roger the Norman two centuries later, it proved a loyal and valiant ally of the duchy of Amalfi, to which it remained linked for the rest of its history. On account of this loyalty it suffered severe damage in 1137, when it was attacked and devastated by the Pisans. The close links with Amalfi allowed Ravello to develop and to prosper, increasing not only the number of inhabitants, but also its own artistic and cultural heritage.

1) Cathedral interior: the pulpit
2) The cathedral

THE CATHEDRAL

The Cathedral stands on Piazza Vescovado and is dedicated to San Pantaleone; founded in 1086 by the first bishop of the town, it was rebuilt in the twelfth century and then renovated in 1786 and again in the 1930's. The very linear façade conserves from the original Romanesque outline three oculi and the window with two lights above the entrance portal. The latter, decorated with a classical marble cornice, has a valuable bronze door made in 1179 by Barisano da Trani: its 54 squares depict saints and stories from the Passion of Christ and two masks. On the right-hand side of the church stands the bell tower, built in the thirteenth century. The interior has three naves (the central one with a trussed roof, the two sides ones with vaults) divided up by ten columns. To the right of the central nave is the majestic marble pulpit, built in 1272 by Bartolomeo da Foggia. The casing, richly decorated with mosaics, friezes and columns, is supported by six slim spiral posts with mosaics, resting on marble lions. The steps leading to the pulpit, on the side towards the presbytery, are closed off by a trefoil door decorated with a mosaic, above which are the figures of the donors, Nicola Rufolo and his wife Sigilgaida della Marra at the sides, and in

3) Bronze portal of Cathedral (1179)   **4) Cathedral interior: the ambo**

the centre the bust of a woman decorated by a tiara which can be identified with the Church or with Sigilgaida. Under the pulpit is a precious thirteenth-century tryptych with a gilded background depicting the Virgin with the Child and Saints. To the left of the central nave, opposite the pulpit, is a fine ambo built in 1130 and decorated with mosaic figures, including Jonah swallowed up and spat out by the sea-monster. In the chapel to the left of the main altar (built in 1643 and restored at the end of the eighteenth century) is the statue with the flask containing the blood of San Pantaleone which liquefies on 27 July, the anniversary of his martyrdom.

VILLA RUFOLO

An outstanding example of Ravello architecture is Villa Rufolo, a spectacular complex formed by the main palazzo (built in the second half of the thirteenth century) and various buildings in Arab-Sicilian style on a wide terrace facing the gulf. Having entered the smaller fourteenth-century tower, we continue along a small avenue flanked by cypresses and reach the moorish Courtyard, decorated with friezes and arabesques, in front of the palazzo, which can only be visited in part. To the left stands the larger tower, probably originally a defence structure. Having gone past the evocative Knights Room, the picturesque belvedere

1) Cathedral interior: the Gospel ambo Marble bust of Sigilgaida Rufolo (13th c.)
2) Statute of S. Pantalone in cathedral
3) Villa Rufolo: lower garden
4) Panoramic view from Villa Rufolo

opens up, a luxurious garden with pines, cypresses and exotic plants: from here it is possible to descend to the lower terrace, also brightened by flowers and exotic plants. Richard Wagner was particularly struck by the spectacular nature of the gardens and saw in it the materialisation of the magic garden of Klingsor in his Parsifal: in his honour each year the gardens provide an evocative setting for a series of musical concerts.

1) Observation point
2) Wagnerian concert

1

2

3

VILLA CIMBRONE

Another outstanding monument is the Villa Cimbrone, built from ancient fragments. The highly original complex is formed by a building with two towers, a courtyard (decorated in the centre by a well) and a Gothic-style crypt facing the sea. Among the many works of art housed here, all different but undoubtedly interesting, two bas-reliefs depicting the Nine Norman Warriors and the Seven Deadly Sins are worthy of mention. The gardens of the Villa are very beautiful, planted with flowers (the rose-garden is particularly fine) and tall shrubs which frame a profusion of statues and small ornamental constructions, including the Mercury (copy of the Hermes at rest from the National Museum of Naples), the

1) Villa Rufolo: The Moorish courtyard
2) Villa Rufolo: The Great Tower
3) Aerial view
4) The cloister
5) Eve's Grotto and statue of Venus
6) Mercury

Venus by Adamo Tadolini in the Grotto of Eve, the Temple of Bacchus, the elegant small temple with a wrought iron cupola and the pavilion of the tea-room. From the belvedere an exceptional view over the gulf of Salerno can be enjoyed.

1) **Temple of Bacchus**
2) **Small temple**
3) **The Seven Deadly Sins**
4) **The Castle and tea-room**

4

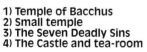

Atrani

The other rock walls standing almost sheer above the sea, at the end of the Dragone valley, seem to leave no space for urban dwellings: yet, it is in this spot that the little centre of Atrani is found. Of ancient and noble origins, it is now a lively holiday resort. Up until '500 Atrani was the most aristocratic of the suburbs of Amalfi. The church of S. Salvatore de' Bireto, with its wealth of history and memories, was the church of the doges of Amalfi: it was here that the person charged with government of the Republic was elected and here it was that the investiture took place, with the placing of the doge's beret (hence the church's name). Finally, the doges were also buried here. The extremely beautiful eleventh century bronze door is the work of Constantinople's finest craftsmen. The collegiate church of S.Maria Maddalena, with its beautiful cupola in majolica dominates a panoramic little square with a wonderful view of the town.

1) **Night scene**
2-3) **Views**

112

1

Minori

Basilica of S.Trofimena, rebuilt in the nineteenth century but medieval in origin has a fascinating crypt and three naves.

The old Roman town of Reginna Minor was also the site of an important arsenal during the golden age of the Amalfi Republic. Today, it is a popular holiday resort with a beautiful beach. From the Roman period are the ruins of a large Villa, dating back to 1 A.D, which encloses a courtyard with a pool in the centre. Some of the rooms are still perfectly preserved, with their vaulted ceilings, frescoes and stucco work decoration. Of great interest is the heating system which is still intact.The

1) Roman villa of 1st century A.D.
2) Detail

3) View and beach
4) Partial view

Maiori

At the end of the great valley of Tramonti nestling behind the enormous beach, lies Maiori, the ancient Reginna Maior as distinct from nearby Minor. Its history, which has Roman origins, is interlinked with that of Amalfi. It was, and still is, the centre of prosperous commercial, artisan and agricultural activity, as well as being a famous seaside resort. The church of S.Maria by the Sea, rising high above the town, stands out with its beautiful cupola and majolica tiling. Around Maiori can be seen the ruins of numerous watch and defence towers - the most noted of which is the Norman Tower, built from the IX century onwards.

1) **Partial view**
2-3) **Views of Maiori**

Erchie

Erchie is a small town, one of those which are usually classified as "minor", but which still offer numerous attractions to those who know how to observe and enjoy their picturesque character. The origins of the town are very ancient, dating back to around the year 1000, when it began to form around the walls of the Abbey of S. Maria de Erchie, built by Benedictine monks around 980 and suppressed in the mid-15th century. The town is flanked by a steep ravine (Sovarano) that winds down from Mt. Avvocata to the sea and the pretty Marina di Erchie beach, a favourite resort of those who enjoy seaside holidays with lovely countryside nearby. Here, the landscape is not lush and verdant as in many other parts of the coast, but is still attractive, with its small rows of vines and citrus fruit groves grown on terraces reclaimed from the wilderness around. The beach is named after a tower built for defensive purpose centuries ago, which still survives today.

1-2) Panoramic views

1

Cetara

The little town of Cetara is charmingly perched on the slopes of a great deep valley. An old sailing and fishing village, it looks out over a little cove, with a tiny port and two cliff framed beaches. In the background, the steep mountain slopes are a sea of green olive and citrus trees. The name comes from the Latin "cetaria", tonnara. Cetara represented the eastern confine of Amalfi's colonies. At the centre of the town stands the church of S. Pietro, which was built in '700. The bell tower, with its primitive medieval shapes, comprises an octagonal cell surmounted by a cone shaped cusp.

1) Characteristic view
2) The beach
3) Fishermen at work

Vietri

Vietri is the last town on the Amalfi coast and enjoys a beautiful position overlooking the Salerno gulf, surrounded by rich verdant vegetation. In the upper part of the town stands the church of S. Battista, with its eighteenth century designs and majolica-covered cupola. To the west of the town, lies the vast and very popular Marina di Vietri beach, with all its modern tourist facilities. Finally, to the north of Vietri, near the hamlet of Dragonea, the Grottoes of San Cesareo offer a fascinating example of the workings of erosion. In one grotto the remains of a little church can still be seen.

1) View
2) Aerial view of seaside resorts

1) View   2) The beach   3) Local dishes

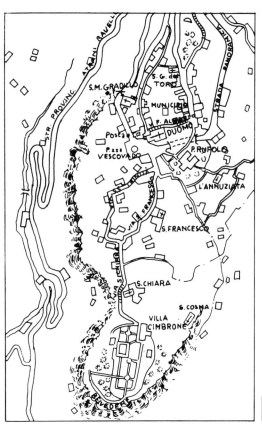

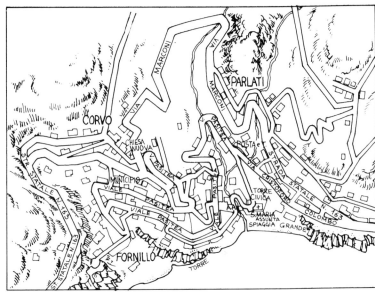

POSITANO

RAVELLO

AMALFI

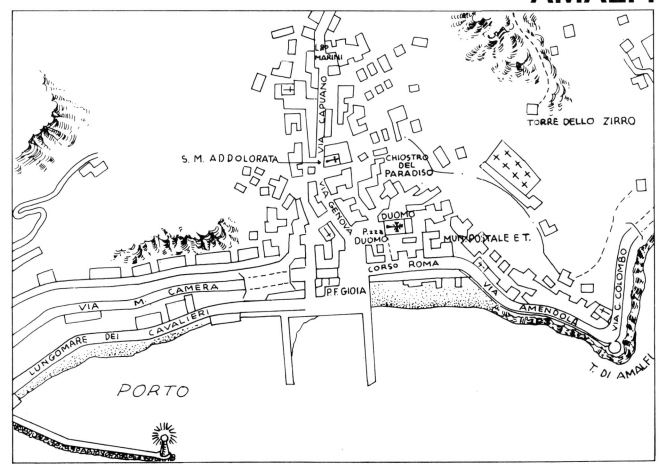

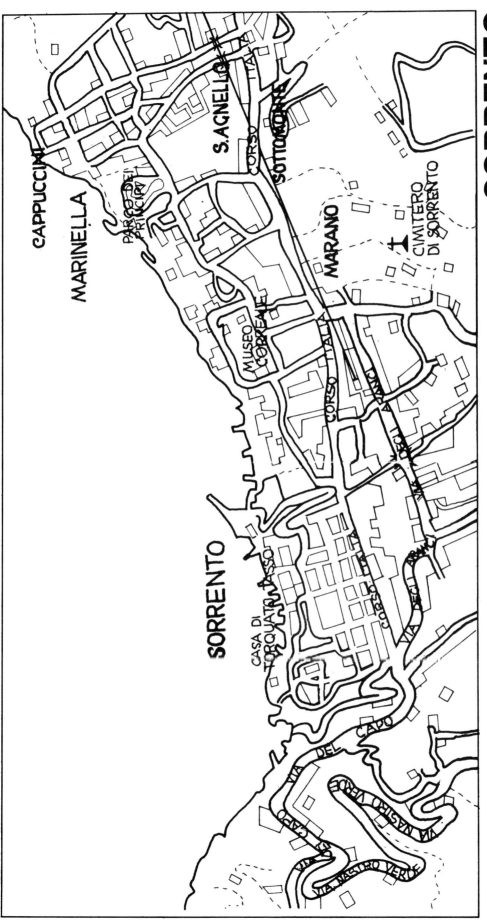

SORRENTO

127

CONTENTS